© Kyle Shields
Thinking Cap Club

This book is dedicated to Kristine
who has endured my flights of ideas
so I could be myself and create.

There once was a dot rolling down a lonely road in search of her friend Art.
"Art, oh Art, where are you Art?" shouted Dot. But there was no answer.
So Dot rolled on . . .

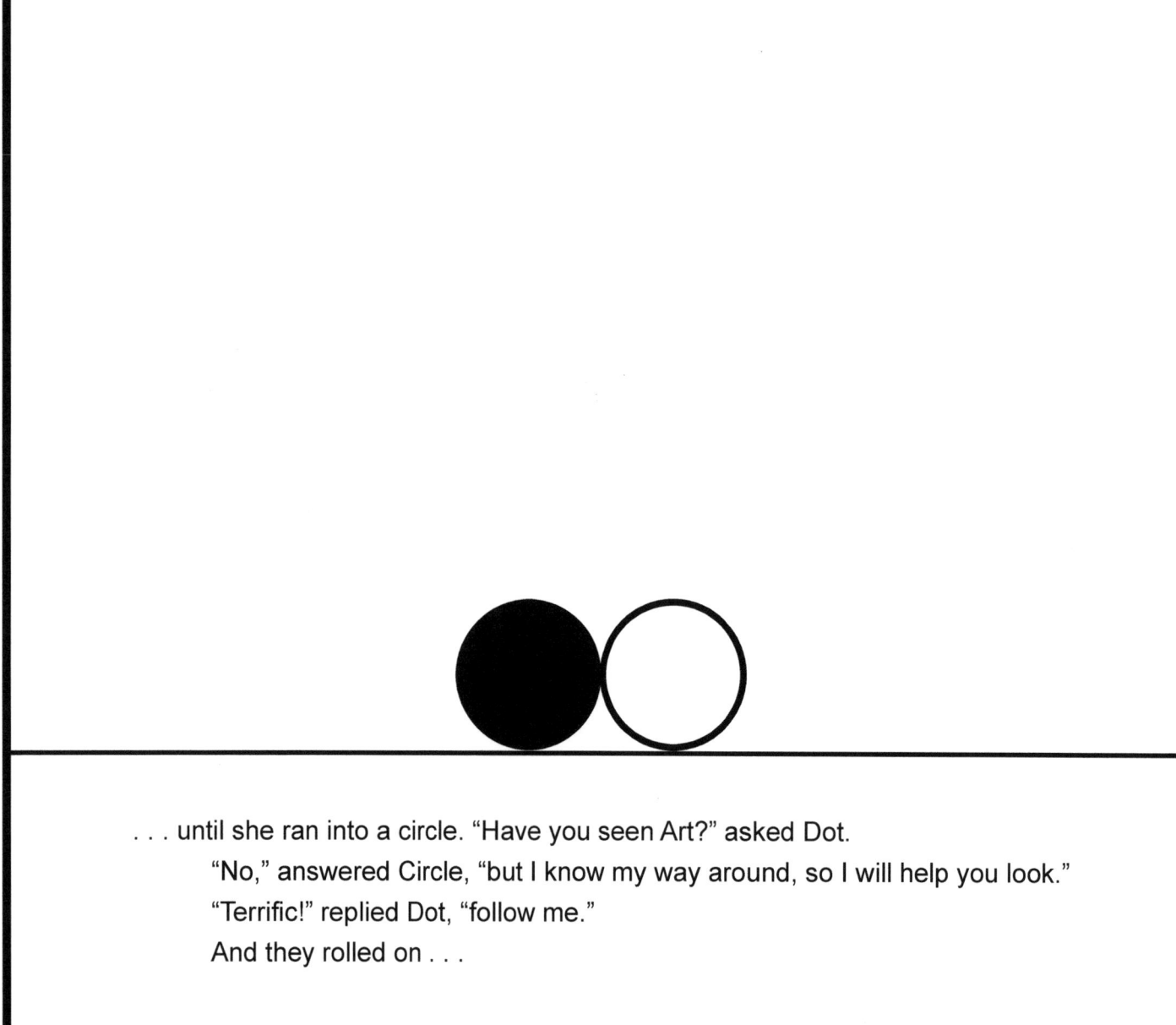

. . . until she ran into a circle. "Have you seen Art?" asked Dot.

"No," answered Circle, "but I know my way around, so I will help you look."

"Terrific!" replied Dot, "follow me."

And they rolled on . . .

. . . until they ran into a line. "Have you seen Art?" asked Dot.

"Why no," answered Line, "but I will come along to keep you on the straight and narrow."

"Then hop on," replied Dot.

And they rolled on . . . and on . . . and on . . .

. . . but there was no sign of Art. They became so angry and frustrated that they started to see Red.

"Have you seen Art?" asked Dot.

"WHY NO!" screamed Red, "BUT I'M VERY BRIGHT, SO I CAN FIGURE OUT WHERE TO LOOK."

"Great," replied Dot, "get on Line."

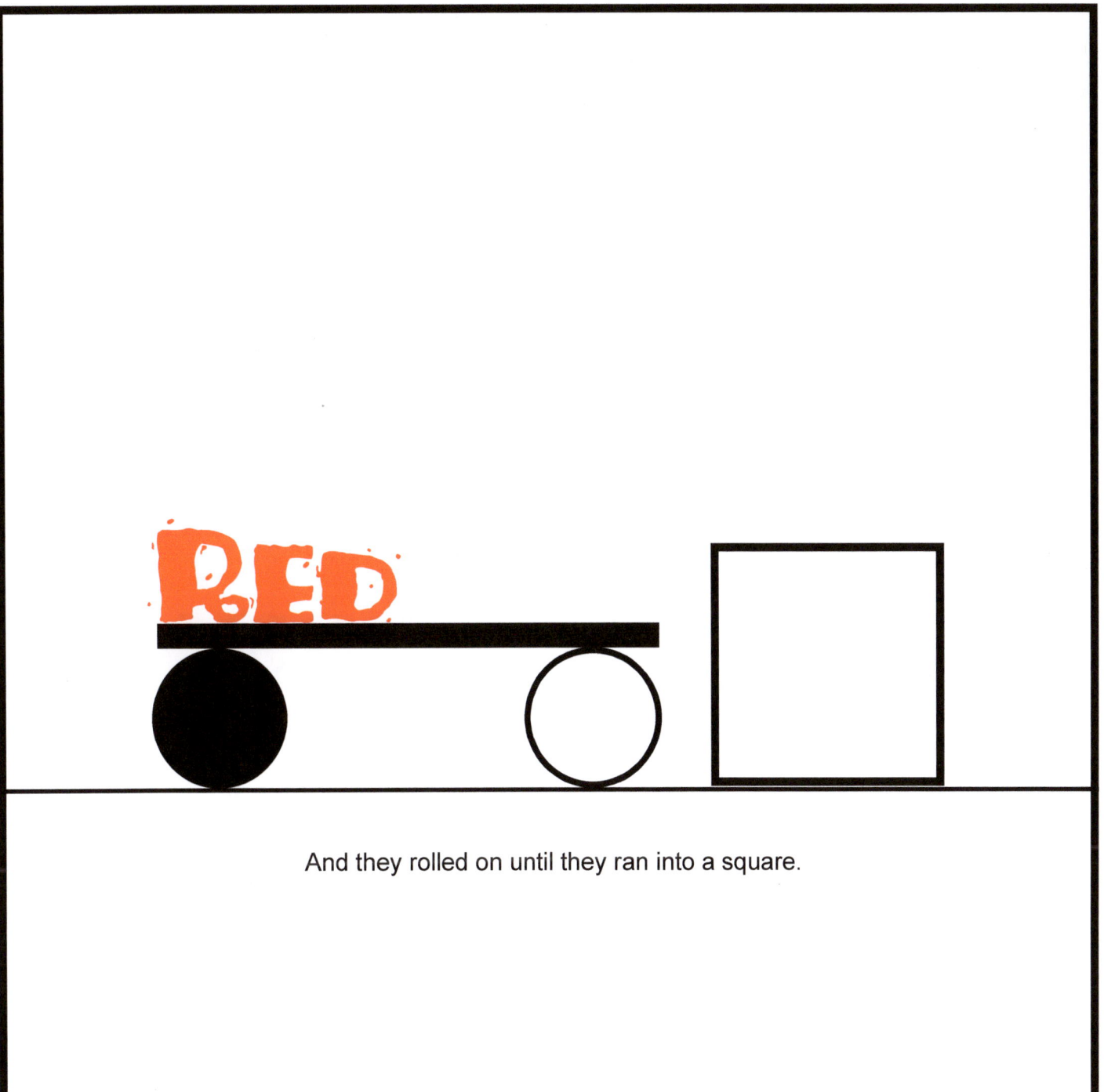

And they rolled on until they ran into a square.

"Have you seen Art?" Asked Dot.

"Why no," answered Square, "but I've been around the block a few times, so I will help you look."

"Square up to Line," ordered Dot.

And they rolled on . . .

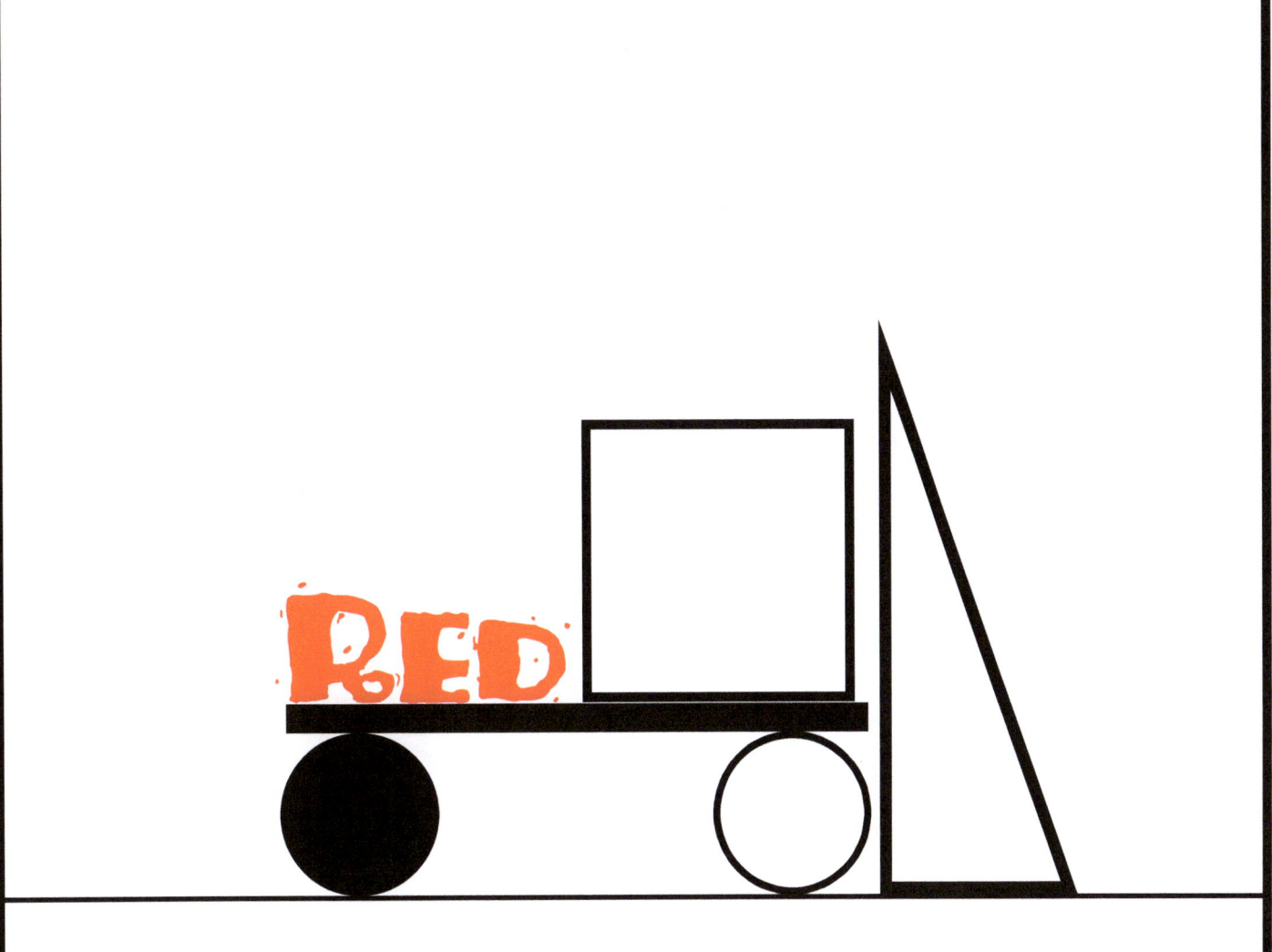

. . . until they traveled up to a triangle. "Have you seen Art?" asked Dot.

"Why no," answered Triangle, "but I can point you in the right direction."

"Make room for Triangle!" announced Dot.

And they rolled on . . .

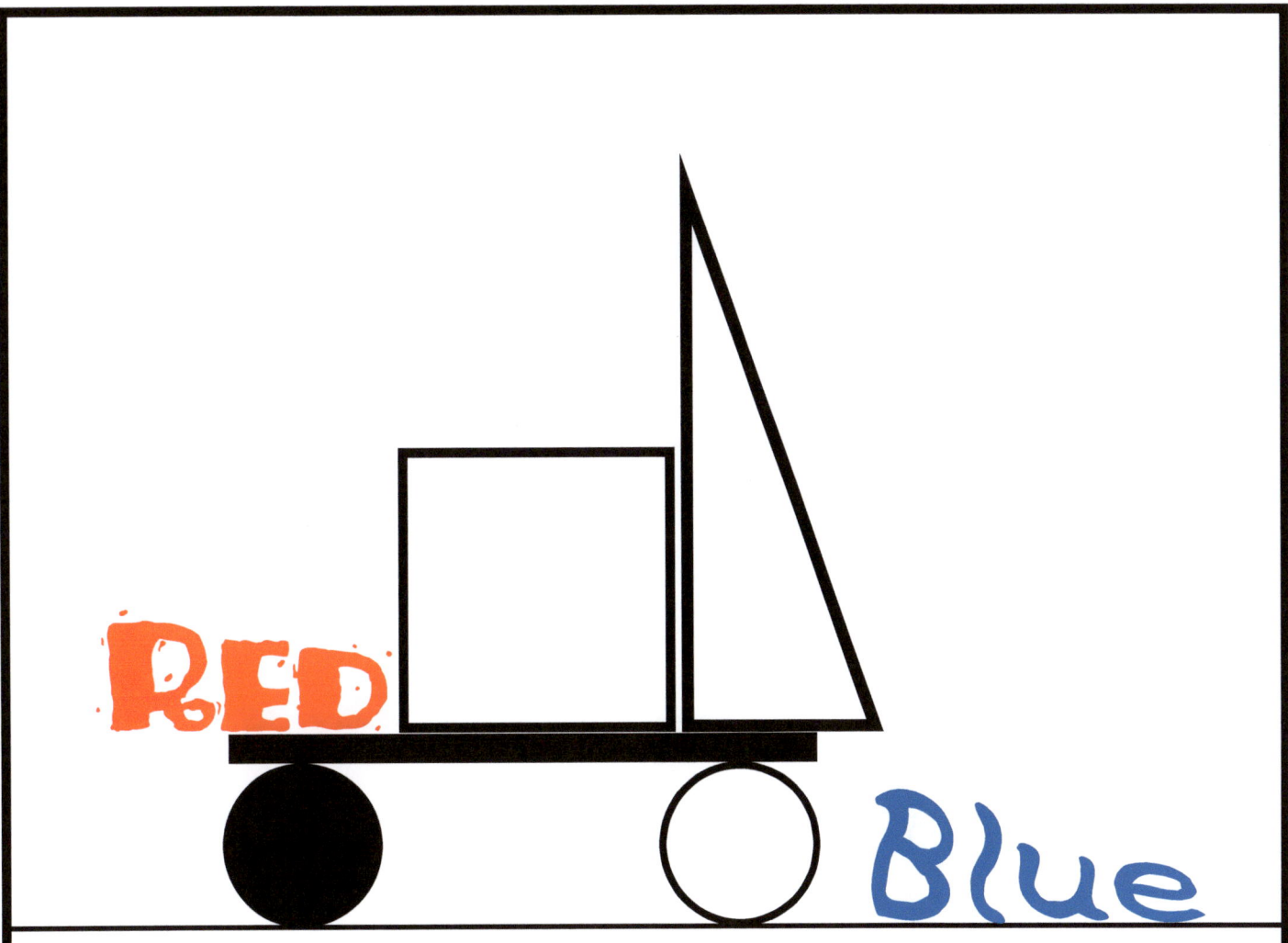

. . . until Blue came into view. "Have you seen Art?" asked Dot.
"Why no," sobbed Blue, "but I'm feeling sad, can I come too?"
"Sure, ride up front in Triangle," said Dot.
And they rolled on . . .

. . . until they zoomed up to a zigzag. "Have you seen Art?" asked Dot.

"Why no," answered Zigzag, "but I can help you look back and forth."

"Great," Dot responded, "but I don't know if we have room."

"NO PROBLEM," screamed Red, "TAKE MY PLACE IN BACK, AND I WILL RIDE INSIDE SQUARE!"
So they shifted around and rolled on . . .

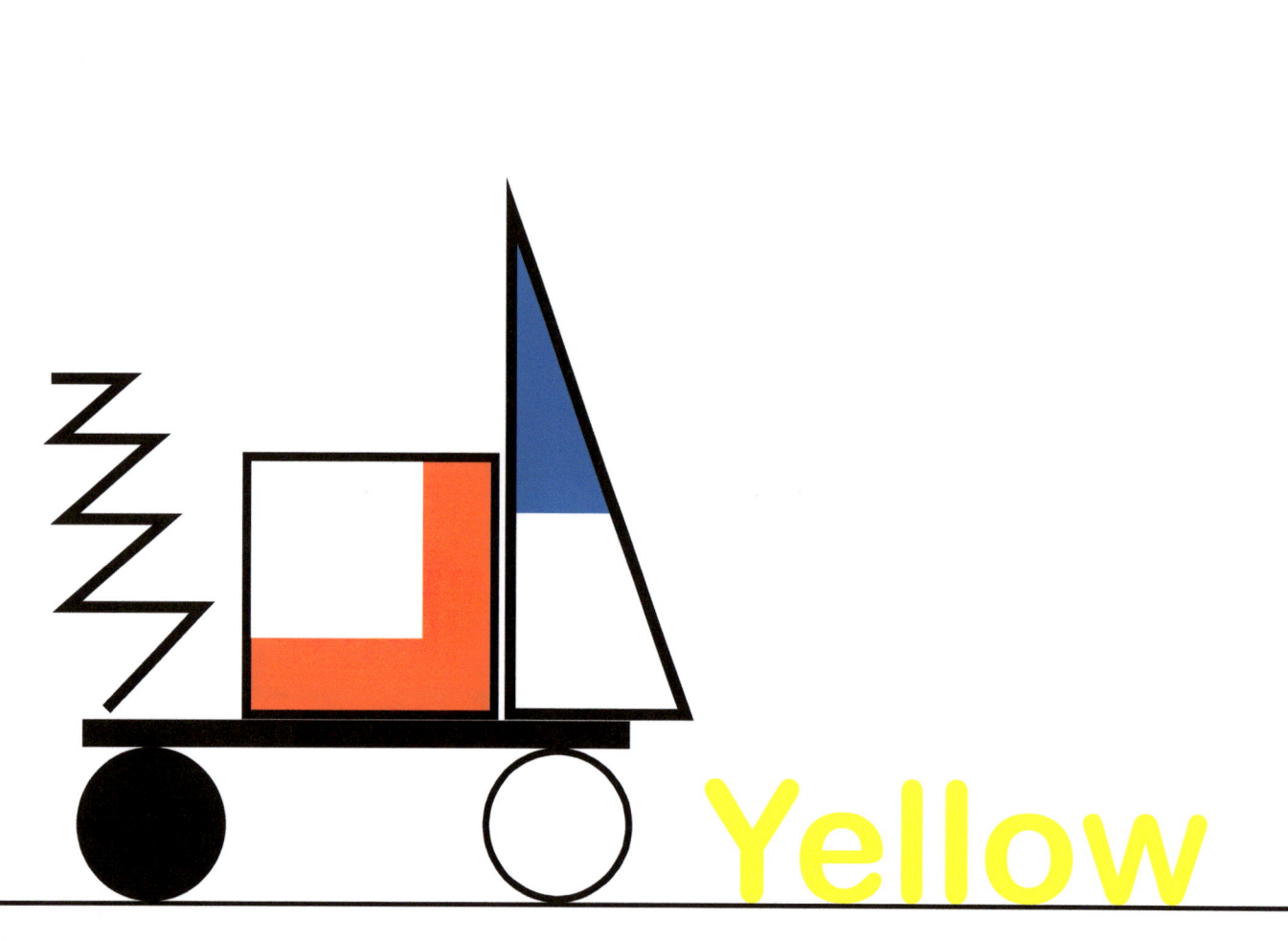

. . . until they saw Yellow, my what a long fellow. "Have you seen Art?" asked Dot.
"Why no," answered Yellow, "but I can light the way in case it gets dark."
"But can you fit?" asked Dot.

Just then, Yellow split in two and let out a yell, "Ow! that hurt." The ow jumped into Circle and the yell hopped in Square. But as soon as it touched Red . . .

. . . Orange squeezed into the picture.
With all three colors in one square they began to feel cramped. So some of Red left to sit in Triangle, but when Red touched Blue . . .

. . . Purple popped out.

Now *two* colors in one triangle is company, *three* is a crowd. So a bit of Blue broke away to share space in Circle with Yellow, but when they touched . . .

. . . Green could be seen.
Now there wasn't room for Blue, Yellow and Green in one small circle. In fact, they were squished so tight that . . .

. . . a small green squiggle squirted out.

And they rolled on . . .

"BUT WAIT!" shouted Red, "I HEAR CRYING."

"It's not me," sobbed Blue. "It's Green Squiggle."

"Please, can I come too?" Squiggle squeaked.

"I'm sorry, but we don't have any ro . . ."

But before Dot could finish her sentence, Squiggle had wiggled his way up and taken a spot next to her.

"I can ride with Dot," said Squiggle, "but don't watch me or you will get dizzy."

And they rolled on . . .

. . . until they came to a bump in the road.
"What should we do?" asked Dot.
"Swerve around it," responded Zigzag.
"No, go straight ahead," said Line.

So they voted on it and straight ahead it was. Up on the bump they climbed.

But with the weight of one dot, a circle, a line, a triangle, a long yellow fellow, Zizag, Square, Red, Green, Purple and a green squiggle . . .

. . . the bump began to bend . . .

. . . and bow . . .

. . . and buckle . . .

. . .and break!

Just then all the colors and shapes began to fall out of control.
Triangle tumbled. Purple plummeted. And Circle sank.

"Help," they all shouted, "we are falling apaaarrrtttt!"

"Did someone say Art?" said a voice, as they fell into place.
"I've been here all along. Staring *you* in the face."